FLYING RED HORSE

ALSO BY DALE MARTIN SMITH

POETRY

American Rambler
Black Stone
The Flood & the Garden
Slow Poetry in America
Susquehanna

NON-FICTION

Poets beyond the Barricade: Rhetoric, Citizenship, and Dissent after 1960

AS EDITOR

Imagining Persons: Robert Duncan's Lectures on Charles Olson (with Robert Bertholf)
An Open Map: The Correspondence of Robert Duncan and Charles Olson (with Robert Bertholf)

FLYING RED HORSE

POEMS

DALE MARTIN SMITH

TALONBOOKS

Talonbooks
9259 Shaughnessy Street, Vancouver, British Columbia, Canada V6P 6R4
talonbooks.com

Talonbooks is located on xʷməθkʷəy̓əm, Sḵwx̱wú7mesh, Stó:lō, and səl̓ilwətaʔɬ Lands.

First printing: 2021

Typeset in Minion
Printed and bound in Canada on 100% post-consumer recycled paper

Interior and cover design by Typesmith
Cover and inside cover illustrations by Ginger Sedlarova

Talonbooks acknowledges the financial support of the Canada Council for the Arts, the Government of Canada through the Canada Book Fund, and the Province of British Columbia through the British Columbia Arts Council and the Book Publishing Tax Credit.

Canada | Canada Council for the Arts | Conseil des arts du Canada | British Columbia | British Columbia Arts Council — An agency of the Province of British Columbia

LIBRARY AND ARCHIVES CANADA CATALOGUING IN PUBLICATION

Title: Flying red horse : poems / Dale Martin Smith.
Names: Smith, Dale, 1967– author.
Identifiers: Canadiana 20210111062 | ISBN 9781772013603 (softcover)
Classification: LCC PS3569.M51695 F59 2021 | DDC 811/.6—dc23

This book is for Mike,
who pointed to Faulkner …

Well, life is just a vapour ...
You breathe it in and what the
heck, it's gone.

—JERRY LEE LEWIS
quoted in Peter Guralnick's
Feel like Going Home (1971)

Flying Red Horse

D-102
MAGNOLIA BUILDING, DALLAS, TEXAS
PHOTO BY PAUL D. CRAVENS
5A-H1682
ADOLPHUS HOTEL
BAKER HOTEL

"Are you a Canadian?" the third said. He had red hair.

"Canadian?"

"He don't talk like them," the second said. "I've heard them talk. He talks like they do in minstrel shows."

"Say," the third said, "Aint you afraid he'll hit you?"

"Hit me?"

"You said he talks like a coloured man."

—WILLIAM FAULKNER
The Sound and the Fury (1929)

In the novel *Absalom, Absalom!* (1936), William Faulkner's fictional character Shreve McCannon shares rooms in Cambridge, Massachusetts, with Quentin Compson. He is also known as Shreve McKenzie in *The Sound and the Fury* (1929) and watches affectionately over the doomed southerner. Shreve, a Canadian, comes from Edmonton, Alberta. He meets Quentin at Harvard in 1910 and graduates in 1914, in time to join the Royal Army Medical Corps, Canadian Expeditionary Forces, in France, 1914–1918. Quentin, born in Jefferson, Mississippi, in 1891, commits suicide by jumping from a bridge into the Charles River on June 2, 1910. Earlier, Shreve acts as intercessor, participating in the telling and hearing of Quentin's familial enmeshment in antebellum slavery, the Civil War, and Reconstruction; he is a medium in the narrative recapitulation of southern honour, violence, and failure. The terror of the continent's legacy is shared by them both.

But why should Faulkner include the Canadian in a novel otherwise so intently concerned with American failures of nationhood and family? Of a distinct region shaped by a reality far distant from Alberta?

~

I could ask, too, why the lyric advance of associations that composes *The Sound and the Fury* and *Absalom, Absalom!* should matter after nearly a century. Seventeen-year-old Darnella Frazier's June 2020 video of George Floyd's murder in Minneapolis by police officer Derek Chauvin drew again to public attention the perennial violence and incongruent relations of race in North America. What is lyric's relation to history, to a public today? How does song appeal to a sense of groundedness in our ungrounded now, in contrast or collusion with images? These questions are rhetorical, though importantly leading. Song has a capacity for brief solace, though never resolution, in an ongoing social and ecological catastrophe streamed 24-7 by the surveillance state.

~

Screens fracture my days. A blankness of the page, and of light. That blanched power radiates through indifferent devices. Surveillance corporations wash out residues of the past. Life occurs moment to moment, in intensities that visually collaborate with our localized bodies. Yet so many of the people I love remain flexible and perceptive despite the assault of machine algorithm. But what labour, what toll on attention ...

Relationships are mixed or erased or elated or divided or stamped blank by terms one might trace back to European habits of self-perception. The European subjective understanding divided the body politic into isolated cells of exchange, distancing self-perception from the flesh and grass and light and air we breathe. The *cogito*, the self, collected pieces, interior distances from grass and oak and warmth of sun or sweat; the labour, the stress of making, doing, opening a world. European violence in the New World begins in distortions of self, in isolating who we are from how we can be in a world with others.

~

Again, a screen. An interface. The light and whiteness, the page. I grew up in Dallas, Texas, on the edge of a previously rural sensibility. Since 1934, a red horse, owned by an oil company, flew over the city. My father, born 1937, adjacent to a small East Texas town, lived the first ten years of his life without electricity. In the city, where so many young, white, previously rural men migrated after the twin assaults of the Great Depression and the Second World War, new divisions were asserted by way of a welcome increase of prosperity. Traces of the emotional stress and exhilaration of that period can be heard in Sam Phillips's Sun Records recordings from Memphis, made between 1953 and 1956. Together, Elvis and his audience staged a fantasy. Greil Marcus evokes how, night after night, that pact served "to replace the world":

> The version of the American dream that is Elvis's performance is blown up again and again, to contain more history, more people, more music, more hopes; the air gets thin but the bubble does not burst, nor will it ever. This is America when it has outstripped itself, in all of its extravagance, and its emptiness is Elvis's ultimate throwaway.[1]

~

When I was in third grade, I became obsessed with country music. I loved the drama, though I could not understand it all. Certainly, the lust and refusal in the music could not fully arrive in me then. But there was a sense of longing I felt in those songs, where there existed a yearning for home. The whining of the pedal steel guitar and the rhythmic tonalities of acoustic and electric instruments drew me intimately into relations inside and beyond the limitations of my body.

~

I drove by the flying red horse with my father on our way to see Charley Pride in 1977 at the Dallas Convention Center. He performed with the white trio Dave & Sugar. Dave Rowland possessed a thick mane of hair and wore an earring in one ear, something I had never seen before. Sugar (Vicki Hackerman and Jackie Frantz), gave the feminine contrast to Dave's macho baritone. The trio had some hits in the seventies, often opening for Pride, and I was enthralled by them.

I listened to Dave & Sugar's version of Shel Silverstein's "Queen of the Silver Dollar," looking closely at the album packaging. Rowlands's unbuttoned western shirt and Sugar's brunette-on-blond appeal reached me sexually in some way I could not then comprehend. Eros and image and song and language striated my attention. It wasn't a hearing only, but a feeling, a complex attunement of senses. I was absorbed by a physical contact with light and sound.

In contrast, the headliner Charley Pride was a Black man singing white music. Critics complained that he should be performing R&B or soul, not white country music. His friend Willie Nelson supported Pride's burgeoning career as a country performer, embracing him with a superlative epithet made famous by Richard Pryor; and though publicly accepted with affection, who but Pride himself can tell what psychic or bodily injury the word inflicted over time?[2] For Pride, Willie helped ensure acceptance for the Black singer's music, leading to big hits: "Is Anybody Goin' to San Antone," "Mississippi Cotton Pickin' Delta Town," "The Snakes Crawl at Night," "Kiss an Angel Good Mornin'."

I did not know about the blank, blanched pages of future screens. The candour of mind and ancestry that measured light against dark. Nothing was ever plainly stated. There was a self-conscious shift of tone of voice when my parents spoke of the evening I spent with my father at the Dallas Convention Center. At least, I hear that shift of voice now in my memory, along with the casual clanking of dishes at supper, the everyday textures of conversation and familial gesture. We were on the edge of so many things I didn't know at the time. Of past rural folkways and new urban spectacles. Of Jim Crow segregation and civil rights cultural change. The lifeways of the country became routinized in submission to new forms of labour, in office cubicles or on retail floors. I took for granted how we lived, how my parents managed, as though it had always been that way. Little did I realize how brief those moments turned out to be, the world slowly disintegrating into an economy.

Charley Pride, who died of COVID-19 on December 12, 2020, is one of only two Black country musicians inducted into the Country Music Hall of Fame. Country music, or country blues, was played before the war by mixed-race performers. Nashville music after 1945 became increasingly a white music. Pride's complex immersion into that scene, after a notable baseball career in the 1950s Negro American League, is remarkable. I was not sure what it meant racially, socially, in 1977 Dallas, Texas. But I felt a distinction, a shift of order, and a welcoming uplift of emotional charge in Pride's voice.

I responded to a sound and a feeling. And to an image. I saw a Black man in blue jeans on the cover of an album. What did it mean to me? How do sound and image and feeling cohere? A Black man's body on the stage in lights contrasted to my small, pale-blond occupation of space in the dark-lit mezzanine of a concert arena.

Pride's physical presence in those lights magnified an image of power challenging what I experienced as self-control and domination. My father's bodily claims through white, paternalistic acts of generosity or occasions of anger radically opposed Pride's expressive range, where tenderness, sympathy, humour, and self-recognition conveyed hope and urgency. His witness to the world in the communal partition of song drew on intensities of feeling that went beyond those I derived through my family. I exposed myself gratefully to his act – as real as life itself.

Pride's skin and his physical features were different from mine and my father's. But his voice was achingly familiar.

It transferred power across bodies, racially complicit in messages of alterity's pleasure. Distance of bodies collapsed in an imaginary where voice, lyric, sound, light played in the kinetic urgency of my experience.

~

I first encountered Faulkner's two early novels during my third undergraduate year of study at the University of Texas. I don't know why Shreve is featured so prominently in those books. The name probably derives from "sheriff." "Shire" (OE *scīr*) and "reeve" (OE *gerēfa*) are compounded over time in that word's etymology to suggest a sense of watching over, or looking out for, the goings-on of a particular region. I hear another origin, too, that may or may not be morphologically accurate, but it conveys a remarkable sounding. "Shrive" (OE *scrīfan* and ME *schriven*) carries into the present a usage of absolution in religious ceremony still active in terms like "Shrovetide" or "Shrove Tuesday," indicating a ritual of purification. Both senses of stewardship and confession seem right in the novels, where Shreve functions as a kind of guardian for his suicidal southern friend. He is, in part, Quentin's confessor.

But in *Absalom, Absalom!*, Shreve also relishes in Quentin's tale of familial decay and brute force. He cajoles his friend, urging him on for more, delighting in wonder at the woven spectacle of words he hears. He prods Quentin to continue the story, implicated by his own consumption of the intimacy between them.

~

In conversation with Quentin, Faulkner's character Rosa Coldfield observes that the pathological Sutpen took "one hundred miles of land" from "a tribe of ... Indians, nobody knows how."[3] But the "how" is important. Although Mississippi had become a state in 1817, the expansion of slavery in the region did not thrive as an economic reality until the 1830s, since most of the area until then had remained in possession of Chahta and Chickasaw peoples. Although Indigenous leaders agreed to the Treaty of Doak's Stand in 1820, Andrew Jackson's signing of the Indian Removal Act a decade later finally succeeded in forcing the Chahta, Chickasaw, Tanêks (Biloxi), and others from their lands. As a result, the mass incarceration and forced labour of people of African descent came late to Mississippi, in 1833, the year Sutpen "took" the area Faulkner fictionalizes as "Yoknapatawpha County."[4]

Quentin Compson is haunted by Col. Thomas Sutpen's familial legacy. The story comes together through often unreliable narration by the likes of the bigoted Rosa Coldfield, who neglects the implications of settlement, not fully revealing how, say, Sutpen, a brutal figure in the novel, arrives self-made after murky affairs in Haiti, another exploited geography in the history of human incarceration and forced labour.[5] I wonder if these books aren't hauntings, talismans? Faulkner looks at the residue and remains, the emotional turmoil and exhaustion of those white settlers who, after the Civil War, retreated into ghostly, violent isolation.

Shreve encounters the force of this violence in Quentin. And is thrilled.

~

I moved with my family to Canada in 2011, which is why, I suppose, I am particularly sensitive to Shreve and his connection to the spectacle of Quentin's stories of human ownership, racial brutality, and the disruption of that world by war. The war signalled an end to a version of overt racist policy. But it did not touch the noetic interior where enforcements of racial segregation required daily scrutiny.

~

A recent meme floating on Twitter recirculates the late comedian Robin Williams's quip comparing Canada to "a really nice apartment over a meth lab" – the United States. It's rare to go a day in public in Ontario without hearing an opinion on the state of things, political and otherwise, regarding the geographic south.

The spectacular, charismatic intensity projected by the United States onto the world is devastating. Most of the world, for a very long time, has only been able to sit by in horror and wonder at the magnitude of U.S. corruption. But who does not profit by its energy and "innovation"? When I lived in al-Hudaydah in the 1990s, it was Michael Jackson and moonwalking that fascinated young Yemeni men, even as Western Policy forced punishing sanctions during the 1990–1991 Gulf War.[6]

~

Eyes cannot be averted from spectacle. The glimmering lights of the flying red horse. Now spectacle is international, a total immersion and dispersal of communal bonds. It does not appeal to our senses in the old ways of persuasion, but through sensation and appetite. Certainly, it is true that the sensual encounter with language has been persuasive since the Sophist Gorgias of Leontini compared spoken eloquence to a kind of witchcraft. But now the sensuousness of text and image separate, become isolated from the weight of self-measure, of logos.

The textures of everyday tingle with sensation-as-meaning. We live in machinery, participating in communicative ecstasy, part algorithmic, part sensuously exhilarating in light, glass, plastic, metal; material soundings felt close to the core, a non-site of no-essence centring called being.

The screen renders its magnitude, shaped and honed by my searches, by my queries, my habits, my consumptions. Another rhetorical question might go here, but the questions are many and inadequate to the situation.

~

The flying red horse in Dallas drew my attention whenever we drove through downtown. Its neon red flashed brightly atop the Mobil Oil Building.[7] Pegasus wings shone against black sky. My eyes, searching for cynosures, the quick glimpse, bright and intense. The animated figure moved according to ground perception, as if flying, guiding traffic toward inevitable destinations.

~

In Shreve I wonder about boundary, division. The border is a fiction where identities mutate briefly in language zones and image zones of affective sensation. What is nation? *We* are not *that*, not of the *States*. The force and features of the negative assert self-protection. Canada's largest trading partner, yes, but there is submission to U.S. surveillance corporations. How else feel into the image zones as sensation orients righteousness, blurring realities, inscribing states of now?

More rhetorical questions, assertions swallowed before adhering as radical claim. But there are no proposals, no solutions, because in the spectacle all is consumed, revealed, detached, or dislocated upon assertion.

~

I asked my mother for a guitar after seeing Charley Pride in performance that fall when I was nine years old. She enrolled me in lessons with Mrs. Boyden. I dutifully applied myself, learning folk songs: "Skip to My Lou," "Home on the Range," "On Top of Old Smoky." Later, I discovered the complex provenance and folkways of these songs. One, "Red River Valley," derived from a Gaelic melody, was taught to me as a Texas cowboy song. But its North American origin is probably derived from encounters in Manitoba between Scots immigrants and Canadian soldiers among Métis communities.[8] The movement of song, and hence of a body of feeling, between nation and region indicates how forms of attachment endure across migratory pathways.

And knowing a young Métis woman probably first sang the song to a departing soldier well before its Tin Pan Alley publication adds a cultural patina to those cowboy voices I hear on the Texas range.

After some time I could move effortlessly between chords. Mrs. Boyden's home was not air-conditioned in summer, a novelty. There was a closeness to the earth. Song. Heat. Voice. Strings. I was a shy singer, but she coaxed me, kindly, into slow expression. Her voice was modelled on Joan Baez's, folky, bright, educated, hippyish. Mr. Boyden wore his hair tied back in a ponytail and built bicycles and sold them from his garage. His son, Brian, my age, met me often after my lessons, and we would build forts or play in the detritus of Duck Creek, a tiny cut of water running behind the Boydens' home. We built elaborate dugouts, covered with branches and debris pulled from the creek. Sand and hackberry and oak. Later, alone in my room in the evenings, I would practise the guitar, learning a kind of mastery over my fingers, moving carefully across the rosewood fretboard.

~

Shreve is a steward to Quentin, and he is affectionate, leaning on his friend for stories. Perhaps he arrives in Faulkner's novels as a better figure of discernment, an outsider with enough detachment to absorb Quentin's stories of charismatic violence, decaying notions of honour, offended pride. But I think it's likely too that Shreve has taken a seat at the show, finding entertainment in the misery and confidence he confronted one cold evening in a Harvard dorm room. Quentin is Shreve's image and voice, a sounding and texture of feeling. They both sit there, in the night, right at the centre of American indoctrination through class education. Boston. Harvard. The Charles River. Both alien to the puritan New England winter landscape that receives Quinten's tale.

~

One thing about the Southern Baptist church I enjoyed as a kid was song, a gratification of sound and movement of voice. As an adolescent, I met Bobby Porter at church, who taught me to play a steel-string guitar, not the classical nylon-string instrument I had learned to play through the generosity of Mrs. Boyden. Bobby Porter played bluegrass. He played a spruce-and-rosewood Martin D-28, with inlaid abalone on the ebony neck, which fascinated me. He taught me to play Doc Watson's version of "Black Mountain Rag" and "Billy in the Lowground." A world of old sounds opened to me. A raw Americana of hearth and field. And the memory of both performed in urban studios.

~

Bobby Porter wore Lee denim jeans and western shirts. He chewed tobacco, and he was elegant and kind to me. He possessed a sense of himself I admired and tried to emulate. Partially, it was the appeal of the music, but also of his image. It mixed with other layers of desire circulating through childhood, of Charley Pride, of folk songs. An elation of body in confrontation with the page, the blank power of communal exchange.

The communication of power forms a central terminus by which other feelings and imaginings find shape and possession. To make music by hand, rather than to receive it in slick packaging, engaged a whole part of my communicative life in song. Lyric arrived in me as I looked through the blankness, the white enmeshed codes of communal time. The sexually transgressive figure of the artist, of white men and women and Black men and women readied my attention to possibilities of beingmeaningbeingnowness.

~

I tell you these things because they compose a personal mythology, and through writing I struggle to ascertain its meaning. I write them to address the blankness, the white strain of the too-familiar residing in so many things now, separated by habits of thought, by surveillance infrastructures, by images and texts detached from stories. How ghosts form and deform, persisting in advance of a feeling. Charley Pride reminds me to listen above and below the vacancy of surface: "Well people may try to guess / The secret of a happiness / But some of them never learn it's a simple thing." [9]

~

There is the sound and smell of earth. Song as mediating potential, through diverse form. When national narratives fail, where personal stories collapse into the socially mediate, I wonder if song might conjure earth back into flesh? Writing provides an opening, but few answers, or none I am capable of discerning. Instead I wonder how poetry works in range of so much that is incommunicable, mute, a driving public force of fragmentation and ruin?

~

Of that ruin, noetic ruin and climate ruin, I worry for my children. I wonder how they see a world that is impossible now to apprehend outside the coordinated structures of ownership channelling inner life? Or it's just the flying red horse again. Illusion and distraction, a monument to the horizontal vacancy of the void. I want to understand permeable relations, to cultivate a generous, lightness of step. "How does a man get to be this way," sings Charley Pride. "Will the timely crowd that has you laughing loud help you dry your tears?" ... "Some people are born to be takers others just wanna give" ... "When people say their life is rough I wonder compared to what." [10]

~

Shreve and Quentin, young men imagined through two novels. They are children brought together from different areas of the continent. Sons and their questions, actual and authorial fathers. The blanched brains of white manhood disturb an ongoing sense of now, of how to be. How I am to myself, to my sons? To others in othered bandwidth image streams?

In the old days, something like prayer or religion might have trained one's attention to local precincts here. But the conserving urgency of poetry finds vitality in temporal *un*restraint. The physicality of breath. How I touch my son's face, embrace my loved ones, share affection. We should laugh easily. Be here, be here. But awareness falters through screens active with images and fragments, gross stupidities and lucid animations. Where are we located? Deliberate contemplation through the rhetorical gesture is replaced with speed and inertia, bound like a DNA helix – tightly, absurdly, wound.

So if the climate collapses, if our skin and genetic obscurities tear the origin of childhood dreams, is it possible to begin again? How to climb out of the human error, the terror, of a faded intimacy? Even if there is hope in song, in story through our affections, even so ...

~

The flying red horse surveyed urban ritual above the Dallas skyline. My eyes searched for it through the dark as it reared over the city. The flying red horse galloped through my imagination, a flashing signal of blank purpose and content only filled by projective eyes. Inanimate witness of light and glass and steel. Modernity's emptiness and extravagance.

~

My desire for Charley Pride opened a pathway. I cannot recall how I registered his "otherness," his Blackness, caught in quiet undertones, gestural authority of voices. His performance was a rare opportunity I greedily held close to me. Songs move through my body, these bodies of feeling sounded into and against imposed conditions of happenstance. It is interesting to think of Charley Pride in rural Mississippi and my father in rural East Texas, both roughly the same age, both in submission to bonds of race and poverty, though conferred differently, neither adjacently nor equally.

~

I recall Charley Pride's version of "Kaw-Liga," a song written by Hank Williams and Fred Rose, originally released by Williams in 1953. It is a story of a "wooden Indian" and the "Indian maid" he loves. Both are mute, made of "pine." Their drama of absurd and impossible love in an "antique store" is comically forced in Pride's 1969 version. I loved it, and asked Bobby Porter to teach it to me, and he did. I can still play the song, feel it in me, its heavy 4/4 beat forcing a mixture of past longings and definite refusals. Pride's uptake of racial play with Indigenous markings and my full adolescent embrace of the song through Pride's voice confer both wonderment and shame in that ventriloquist act. Along some borderland that is not geographic but temporal, where the spectacle of North American postwar experience disintegrates, I see bodies in conflict and submission to unforeseen interiors.

~

Despite violent upheavals in everyday life by spectacle mediation and illusion, communication thrives.[11] Each flash and figure compels awareness, anticipates action, increases threshold potentials. The New World began with spectacle and communication, thrilling reportage.

Quentin to Shreve: "What I learned was that there was a place called the West Indies to which poor men went in ships and became rich, it didn't matter how ..." [12]

"All right," Shreve said. "Go on." [13]

Shreve adheres to spectacle in his blanched screens of mind, pressures, successes, survivals. Experience arrives not blank but spectral full, ghostly wild with the possible other seeing, hearing, moving, sensing. Red Pegasus above a city skyline.

NOTES

1 Greil Marcus, "Elvis: Presliad," in *Mystery Train: Images of America in Rock 'n' Roll Music* (New York: Plume, [1975] 2015), 117.

2 See Charley Pride and Jim Henderson, *Pride: The Charley Pride Story* (New York: William Morrow and Co., 1994); Joe Nick Patoski, *Willie Nelson: An Epic Life* (New York: Back Bay Books, 2009); and Joe Bargmann's interview with Pride in the *Dallas Observer*, July 5, 2016, "Will Darius Rucker Break Country Music's Color Barrier Once and for All?" Richard Pryor's eponymous 1968 debut album and his 1982 release *Supern******* are probably sources for Nelson's epithet.

3 *Absalom, Absalom!* (New York: Random House, [1936] 1990), 10.

4 See Ned Sublette and Constance Sublette, *The American Slave Coast: A History of the Slave-Breeding Industry* (Chicago: Lawrence Hill Books, 2016), 411 and 449.

5 Faulkner's genealogical note on Sutpen reads thus: "Born in West Virginia mountains, 1807. One of several children of poor whites, Scotch-English stock. Established plantation of Sutpen's Hundred in Yoknapatawpha County, Mississippi, 1833. Married (1) Eulalia Bon, Haiti, 1827. (2) Ellen Coldfield, Jefferson, Mississippi, 1838. Major, later Colonel, —th Mississippi Infantry, C. S. A. Died, Sutpen's Hundred, 1869." See *Absalom, Absalom!*, 307.

6 And now "innovative" American war manufacturers sell weapons to the Saudi government who uses them again against the Yemeni people in an extreme and ongoing human crisis. For more on the seven-year-long conflict, see "Yemen War: No End in Sight" (March 24, 2020), an online article by Amnesty International.

7 The Magnolia Petroleum Building opened in 1922; it was the tallest structure west of the Mississippi, and it was air-conditioned. Standard Oil acquired the company in 1925. Standard's trademark Pegasus was added to the building in 1934. By the time I was born, 1967, Mobil Oil had assumed ownership of the company, the building, and the sign.

8 See Canadian folklorist Edith Fowke's "'The Red River Valley' Re-Examined," in *Western Folklore* 23.3 (July 1964).

9 Ben Peters, "Kiss an Angel Good Mornin'," performed on *Charley Pride Sings Heart Songs*, RCA Victor LSP-4617, 1971.

10 See Charley Pride's performances of Max D. Barnes, "The Man I Used to Be," on *Country Feelin'*, RCA Victor APL1-0534, 1974; Ted Harris, "Crystal Chandelier," on *The Country Way*, RCA Victor LSP-3895, 1967; and Glenn Martin, "I'm Just Me," on *I'm Just Me*, RCA Victor LSP-4560, 1971.

11 See David Levi Strauss's *Co-Illusion: Dispatches from the End of Communication* (Boston: MIT Press, 2020).

12 *Absalom, Absalom!*, 195.

13 *Absalom, Absalom!*, 205.

In the Exchange

IN THE EXCHANGE

Filled the hours of today
with many obligations.
Paused a moment with
the trash, icy and tight
to see light snow in orange
street glow. A car
pulled up to the curb.
The guy who collects
recycling rummaged
through cardboard for
bottles and cans. My footprints
from earlier had faded
under a white expanse
of new snow. Absolutely
uneventful as language.
The many traces of words
lost, unvoiced
in stillness.
We are it, I guess
in the dark garbage
calm of a week's remains.
Mexican parrots are dim
in my mind. The president
of all the globe somewhere
grows calm as a babe
in a madness of who
owns and doesn't. The man
finds my empties, clanks
a bag around to his car.

Dear winter deities, let us go,
believing in fragile exchange.
Merchants covered the ocean
bloodied the Saint Lawrence.
The Great Lakes of the North.
In manic disposition, their law
imposes sanction. For once
it could just be quiet
in dissension. I like
the sound the snow makes
under my feet. I listen
to it squeak. I feel the inconstant
slippage. The cold
stings my arms.
Another day and nothing
in the full dark after dinner
isolate remains.

THE TIME OF THE NOW

for Roberto

Tonight, quiet. Snow
goes to ice in the air's
cold skein. No, it's the skin
of earth's malleable mould.
Or a stillness shifts
under cloudless, starry
sky crusty chill. It's old –
the sentiment – archaic
attention to ground, to
insoluble atmosphere.
Streetlights press an eerie
orange on the gloam –
one of those Old English
poeticisms, glowering
in the ongoing modern
devastation of the now.

IN TIME

for R.J.

1

Teakettle steams on wood stove
I like voices when the room
folds in, words like light
dim in the south window
revenants here, things I've seen
where I've been led to
self from holy seeds, and now see
in fussed, faded vantage
friends, like trees, painted
canvas, stringed
out-of-tuned instruments
hang on a post by the stove

2

In branches night sky blackens
red oak and ginkgo, lettuce, onions
humble vegetation, the years
in objects collected, shown
by the light of the room, photos
of Harvey and Barbara, time's long
ghosts hang in the lamp's dim
scrim of blankest identity, a solid
outline that one time lived extraordinary
the movement here, hurdy-gurdy
tempo, spectres recollected in beat
solidarity, o mid-winter empty
personify the briefly pretended
continuous presence of our making

EVERY DAY YOU

Every day you
look for surprise
in the ordinary
routine of now.
An awakening
through the noise
shows what's light
and readied
to be known,
your own ongoing
ground. And on
you return like
a musical pattern.
On to the sound.
On in the round
of days to play
in, as if a child
wilded the lost
and the found
the weird and the
blatant beat.

EVERYBODY OUGHT TO TREAT A STRANGER RIGHT

1

Vision isn't seeing, and blinded
the voice tears through Beaumont/
Dallas 1930s hot that sound
gospel tense God laid out
the road you're on, set
on fire, you, stranger
sit, sound a lyric thrumming
Willie Johnson

2

Barrel-chested testament
expands the cracked heat
vocal strange, and appears
not single, nor personal –
pierce, then, the mask, one
measures oneself – created – Adam's
face the dark sees through
"God Don't Never Change"

WRECK ON THE OLD HIGHWAY

Hang around, Daddy. Woods and
fence line guide the highway.
He was born working, down and out.

And robbed molasses, or
stole the colours, and
tore the feathers, ate

pork fat, hominy
gravy, rattlers, green
pastures cleared by Haitian

traffic, a manse, Chahta
trails, highways engulfed by
flame, and ransomed

human dignity from machine
code, that refusal
hymnal and song

the human bone
cagey
seeing, and take

privilege as mercy's
cowed bulk, the meat
and grain, they are eyes

what sees through, blank
holes, ghost toys ache
invisible, outreaching

SUN AND RAIN

Sun and rain, sun and rain.
All afternoon. Now
                Sonny Terry
twists the room.   Window
greenery and goldenrod. Like
                        wonderment stampeded
what I remember
                I am – blank day's sudden
storm. Frequencies attuned to character
or person – mask – sounding
                another order in the stamped rhythm.
From somewhere in evening
                        memory – church
or porch song. Living suddenly
vivid seeing what it was to be
                the one doing
all the talk, all the acts of all the daily
goings-on.   Flip the record
                fold the clothes.
Sun and rain all day long.

OPENINGS

Leaves yellow and fall in the new fall air.
        Emery Glen, Little Hat Jones.
Spruce-top acoustics, breaking voices
        syncopate accounts of custom.
Sound travels north on the Mississippi.
        A blues modernism, moaned
and bent from cartel logics, human
        supplement. Lonnie Johnson.
Buddy Moss. A string-stutter impulse
        spectre in the voice, a broke
entrance or what loss looks like above.
        Compose guttural rhythm
folk lightning strum and local
        timbre. Falling in the new
fall air, recorded density of time
        open again, open now.

LIGHT SHINE

Music lived inside me
desiring outside sound-time
loss tempo grieve
gone memory long ago
the old oil building
brute cotton sugar days
take away the person and all
the people come out
crows' feet my mother said
corner of my father's eyes
car tires on asphalt black
sky light red horse red horse
exchange place and person
and all those masks
dance extravagance
vocal fields all night
light shine

SHREVE

I used to walk with my son to his dojo
I'd sit there on a black vinyl sofa that smelled
of other boys and men while he
used his body on the mats with kids his age
I tried to read, looking up, looking down
my glasses moist in the humid gym
I wanted to figure something out about
Canada and my being here from Texas
What were the differences? Where
did nation intersect? Faulkner's Shreve
got me thinking about past life
in the southern USA and how the alien
Canadian Shield yielded such weird
rocky yellow pine organic jagged density
of place, and white European-descended
Protestant folks and Jewish people and
Caribbean and Haudenosaunee and
prairies mountains oceans Arctic ice
there is no ground no person no thing
Shreve is character charisma
invented by American looking
Shreve presses on in disbelief for more
story in the exchange
huddles next to his American friend
one cold Cambridge night listening

West Indies ships signalling
harvest routines common mean
discover no bottom to desire
My son tugs my arm
Did you see me? he said
I won the spar the other
boy laughing next to his father
Lowered my book, said hello to him

THE DREAM ELECTRIC

Shaking leaves and blossoms
Pickering and Darlington just south
Lake Ontario, driving the 401 –
deciduous greenery. Divided
in machines of convenience and delicate
uncertainties of material life, the highway
is stalled with holiday traffic. In a time
before me or you, a quiet like crickets or running
water textured the everyday. As if time never began
melting ice, species die-off.
In grain or meat, fleshy protein, we
kill things or possess them. Invent
motors, fuel rods, cool a radioactive
stew. Like dreams of mythic
creatures swimming open-eyed in emerald lumen
to warm our nakedness. The romance
of utopian dalliances and free soil transits
destiny, or just plain history. The plant
steams electric. Carolinian woodland
home to warblers and red-winged blackbirds
predates the human idea.
I've gambled in England and in Spain
lonesome, the cuckoo.
Little white churches. Clean fields.
The energy of things released
by sunlight, the maiden, a virgin
dynamo luxuriant. Google the World
Fair, 1900, Henry Adams.
Cathedral buttresses and cinquefoil

cruciform transepts. Abstract
force of piston and steam. Believe
rapid telepathy. Shamanic
handprints stained in limestone.
The ancient chemical, the chimeric
charm, fuelling up in Frontenac.
Narrowing distances.
Wind and light and sky.

April *
Ontario

Nothing is real.
Nothing is certain.

—WERNER HERZOG
Cave of Forgotten Dreams (2010)

How is it crows
go about with such a fuss
shaking white
pines, laughing
in common
appetite – alert to delight
in the play and fray
of their dailiness?

~

It began as a Sunday walk
to the lake with my sons
the oldest beside me
(the other had run ahead)
turned and said, Papa,
why is the earth warming –
this is wrong, the sudden
early April of
Ontario?

~

Do you know how quickly
Yukon rivers vanish
– the Kaskawulsh Glacier
violently shifting
its fluid density?

~

I tried to comfort him
– we walked in a kind of
embrace, and all I could think
with ironic plunder,
Why do you weep
in warm April air
going to the park
in the calming breeze?

~

When I'm dumb to self-
doubt, gassing
a rental or jetting
over the continent
I give myself
to the standards of travel –
so what might it mean
giving up the comfort
of speed?

~

The presidential tweet
circulates in the ambient
commune of machine
connectivity, and I wonder
if there is time
for the quiet house
finch searching seeds
of grass in urban yards?

~

What if every day
a time machine
poem reminded
how words are
doors that open
what it meant to live
by ochre and manganese
interior flame vision?

~

In the movie by Werner Herzog
about caves there are hands
of Shamans and many paleo-
lithic animals are seen
after the dark of millennia
in a flickering of filmic
illusion, and I wonder
how it really might have been
so far away from us now?

~

Is there time
to pick a side –
to see the art
in bird politics
like hiking in a field
where my skin
warms slowly
by ancient sun rhythms?

~

Who seeks
the Irrawaddy dolphin
or the tiny Bramble
Cay melomys, even
Hawai'i's yellow-
faced bee?

~

I have looked
to language as a way
to coordinate my doubt
by an ongoing
interrogation, but
do these questions
require answers, a sense
or knowing that explains
walking to the lake
with warm sun
on our skin
in early April?

~

How does speech accommodate
liquid disorder – a strain
of routine pulses, habits – endless
cuts in languid
genome sequences?

~

Aren't words like ghosts
inhabiting host
assimilators, kinetic
revenants slipping
in and out of
bodily needs?

~

I wonder, too, how
lyric intones
prophetic resonances
of the cognitive function –
how might I let myself go
for instance, beating
to the heart
of questions
I'll never know?

~

What do I recall
through memory when I see
a flying red horse
on the Mobil Oil Building
downtown Dallas
marking the burning
of fossil fuels?

~

Isn't it like a dream
searching the night sky
for a glimpse, a sighting
of Pegasus, birthed
in the blood of Medusa?

~

Aren't dreams spectacular
in their distant origins
moving old tales through
new soundings and awakenings?

~

And what did I want
poetry to bring
against a debris of
progress
where webs
of feeling in April
heat provoked my son
to despair?

~

Wasn't there a kind of
glory in poetry's hard
landing, antithetical
and homespun like
Ariadne's unwinding?

~

That image of Theseus
deep in the maze
of the bull, and Herzog's
bison in Chauvet Cave
startled me, so I ask
how should I receive
the ancient message –
vivid dreamlike
animations of
prehistory?

~

I wonder, too, what happened
to the Saint Helena olive
the American chestnut, the bastard
gumwood – trees gone or on
the way to extinction?

~

I am dismayed by the depletion
of species and receptive
to far records of ochre and bone
instruments, and I wonder
why should I uncoil
to sound or image
mysteriously – how might I
wander, play matter's
mantras, breathe
into the made-up
origins of words
going out?

~

I worry, and ask
how does one
locate the least
flycatcher, a tear
in the airy infinite
where I dream?

~

I watch Herzog's
questioning of
experts and cave
scholars, and I wonder
how can it be
the screen's light
like juniper wicks
flames with an intensity
of the sun, the very one
warm now in the April
air of Ontario?

~

Recently I saw
a car-flattened sparrow
when I waited for a bus
as it rained
on dismal grey
feathers and little
exposed bones –
and how did this feel –
what did it call out of me?

~

Was I thinking
about Gorgon
blood and how
myth embodied the Pegasus
in red neon?

~

I often wonder, too
if time is even real
by any measure – like
how is it the past sees
straight through me and why
does the future drive
against my inward certainties
with such apparent
contradiction?

~

I worry because it's weird
how languages disappear
like Bramble Cay melomyses
and I can't soothe my son
in warm April lake air –
these days how could it be
one does not weep
with the arrival of spring?

~

Wittgenstein said
"If we take eternity to mean
not infinite temporal duration
but timelessness, then eternal
life belongs to those
who live in the present" –
and I hear these words offered
to direct a kind of self-measure –
for isn't time approached
both as bodily duration and
also as an experience
of consciousness?

~

To the inner life
is it not true
we move forward
and back in the
detritus of living?

~

Experiences and knowledge
cohere or divide
over an immense spectrum
of recall and sensation
so how is it also not
possible from our personal loci
to map extreme boundaries
of imagination that seem
almost to reach the infinite?

~

And isn't the moral
density of our connection
to the world somehow
distilled by images first
and words then come
by tongue and ink
to realize an immense
division?

~

Once when I saw a forty-
thousand-year-old
vulture-bone flute
in Tübingen, I wondered
how did it sound
and what tongue, what
beat accompanied
breath in the passage
of song?

~

As if somehow
a part of ourselves
resides elsewhere
aerated in social
commons – the ongoing
dints and dings
of the daily?

~

I tried to listen
across a density of time
as if to dream
song's prophecy
but what in the silent
airless, glassy
encasement of the flute's
display did the image
recall in me?

~

Can it be what I
don't know works
to achieve its clarity
by word and image
in shape and sound
walking to a park
in spring lake air?

~

Why had I wanted to solve
problems of my friends
and family, seek
new ways of thinking
of the least
flycatcher, the Saint
Helena olive?

~

Could it also be our bodies
grow incoherent
even as throughout the eco-
imaginary of our being
Ariadne still traces a pathway
in the stony mazes
of the Minotaur?

~

The flute, the cave, the maze –
bison and tigers, small
horses, rhinos –
do I not follow a threaded
sound-image anterior
to speech – looped
into a kind of recurrent
measure?

~

Isn't extinction a promise
of supplication
at the aperture
of the maze?

~

Or in this domain
of the biological given
how far am I
willing to see?

~

What is it about
the cave and the maze
the dark and the quick
fuse, projected
bulls and aurochs
on limestone walls
of the great hall?

~

Isn't the material
temporally frozen
even as red and
yellow ochre stains
and black manganese
appear to reach out
from the infinite
without even traces
of the modern
sense of testament
in Lascaux and
Chauvet Caves?

~

What if words come
late and planted
in the bloody
brain stem to
entangle threads
of passage?

~

How is it crows
go about with such a fuss
and my boy weeps
in the unseasonable
warmth of his
dailiness?

~

I wonder too about the impulse
to tell a story – how find
lyric openings in the out-
of-ordinary routines
of the social animal
(if by social we mean
a connection to others
and to things)?

~

In poetry, aren't words
antithetical and homespun
stranding readers purposely
in the maze – or hidden cave –
in the antique dark
and human patina
of an inhuman fray?

~

I mean, can there be
a lightness of a flying
red Gorgon horse
external to the cave
and the maze, the web
of string and hazy
makeshift crazy
of the modern
meme jam-up
tweet show?

~

Is it not a question
of lyric and tale
like painted skin
taut on the hollow
drum where sound
pinches loose in dark
interior air?

~

Do images of living things
like the dusky seaside sparrow
linger in an afterlife
so deeply wounded
no words, no actions
resolve a terror
of extinction?

~

What conveys an interior
wild along mazy
genome sequences?

~

Maybe in the time condensary
the Pinta Island tortoise
swims to sea and we
eagerly advance
from bone to flint to steel –
wax, papyrus, ink, and light –
Gutenberg, Xerox, Google?

~

Maybe being in the intersecting
loci of two times
has much to do
with a sense of my being
haunted by intruding forms –
sparrow or flute, a sudden
turning of my son to me
demanding light or string
at the coiled terminus
of the maze?

~

Maybe it's a feeling of being
watched like when I wake
from a dream and look for a way
to describe an experience
in an accompanying frame
identical according to
what I see sleeping?

~

So how continue
when I take hot tea
entering routines
of toast and making
ready the day
the cave I enter
while the dream resists
easy entry to my lips?

~

I want to say it will be okay
that our time here now
matters in all the old ways
but haven't I come to a point
of intersection, another
unwinding or recoiling
on my way to the park
with my son, like many
fathers have walked
with their sons
by Lake Ontario?

~

Nothing so simple as
"no answer," that shameful
pride in the ineffable
gnomic utterance – instead
I wonder in the fray
of these perceptions
how to deliver
an ideal resistance
to meaning and doubt
and thereby open
oneself
to what comes?

Sons

Spiny lizard on yucca

Bury spade tip in clay

Scoop it watch him

Scrape with plastic toy

The ground gives

Slowly

Loosen its roots

With water

Pat warm dirt and mulch

Hello Tree

Hello Tree

Hello Tree

His hand on you

Asleep and darkness

Where no moon tonight

Breathe him in

Chocolate milk drips

From table to floor

Over apples I cut

Tears come and his little

Dance of frustration

It's okay

It's okay

Morning in curtains

Light on my pages

And kiss

Soon to grow
A bow and arrow
In his hands
My cowboy
My dragon
The cars spin
On a circle
Of roadway

Play catch-the-moon
Children laugh as handfuls
Of pecan moon and sycamore
Pod stars scatter
From the sky's dark
Bouncing on the dusky
Vinyl trampoline

Show them

A man

What that could be

Sweeping scarecrow

Hay off the porch

Fall moon blank

Blue sky runic

Figures of cloud

Barely made out and the black

Wingspan of an owl

Lows under the boughs of

Hackberry hedge

A sound

In him pulls

Out of his skin

Climbs a tree

Are you able

To be in these roles

And absorb

That look

Of their sweet eyes

And go with them

And come back

New again

No bears no lions
Not even the clouds
Hold forms
We can name
Against the terror
Of a second
Coming
That darkness
And pressure
Warm hands
His breath
On my cheek
At night
The error
Of the mind's
Indifferent
Observance
Of signs

Soon we go

Home

Home

Where we are

To play in the swaying

Shade of late day

When I come home

Bare feet

On pink gravel

Wagon and tricycle

My cave mind

Arranged in the play

Of my boys

These children and

Going west

The sun

Walk cold surf

Bare feet in grey

Tide coming in

Golden Gate

In mist while pelicans

Glide to the surface

We are watching

Them come and

Go along headland

Dunes and tourists

Stand by a dock

My arms heavy

With him moving

The cut

Of his face

On me

Soon it will end

The plane goes up

It is sucking

Three hours

After security

In the air

Over the West

We see clouds

Against window plastic

In the tedium

Wobble

Piss into stainless steel

Bowl and blue anti-

Bacterial liquid

Wipe hands

On our jeans

They are here
And dying too
Call it entropy
Or whatever
Will you deal
With this fact
Tell them
When it comes
Goodbye
And go inside
With the rest

A kiss

Goodbye

Goodbye

A kiss

These days

In a book

Far away

In the dusky

Homecoming

Of our post-

Human

Hearth

We look

For home

And go

On pretending

It's a place

On a map

But no map

Retains

The heat of it

He falls

Or a furry caterpillar

(Blackish – yellow)

Stings with sharp points

And enters bodily

Disturbing the substance

Of memory

Watch him

Hold a China-

Berry branch

By the house

Where neighbours

Play with their kids

And the damp buggy

Fall mosquitoes pester

Drink a beer

To keep cool

Words

No answers

To the question

Naked flapping

Penis in the cold

Of morning

Watch them

Watching *Sesame Street*

We are here

We are here

It’s not enough
And that’s okay
Home happens
Perfect and
Strange in its
Mobility
Inside the wild weird
Writhing of sleep
Hungry forms
Twisted on the floor

We ran around

In the new backyard

Gravel under our toes

New oak growing

On ragweed

The boys quarter

Vietnamese

Nearly naked

In north wind

Hold him these

Cold nights

Never close

Enough

Never thought

Forms could hold

So fast

And what is it

We are bonded to

New jeans and a blue

Chambray shirt cowboy

Boots and a leather belt

Holding the Chinaberry

Balanced like an ape

Parrots flew by

We were dressed in warm clothes

And coloured scarves

Covered the youngest

Penguin cap on his brother

Sunlight on soft leaves

Evergreen shade by the fence

We dumped mulch

Swept the trailer

Ate bean tacos for breakfast

Late they sleep
And the dark house
Sounds the sleeping
They drift in dream
Wind out the window
My bare feet on cold floor
Waking he moans out
And sleep again
Comes to the house

I remember how distinct
From birth each
Movement of limbs in air
Gulping breath
To reveal the pitch
Of what each is
Apprehended by appetite

Halloween

Skeletons dance

By the images of

Dead pets

My son

Naked in morning

Brightness

Yellow leaves spin

In the grass

How much of you

In them leaves

The urgency of past

Generations

Taking up

The broom he is

Sweeping straw

Off the steps

A moment in him

Almost medieval

In acute vividness

Of form

Their eyes are big

In candlelight and

Birthday cake

Glows in the dark they

Sing and delight in

Mystery of rituals

Urging us to achieve

Our roles

What is it you want

In you to bet

What can be said

Against all that can't

In them they measure

You by a cast

Of metaphor in

Genetic thrusts

Of creature love

Formed by the stress

And relief of play

Show them a man

You will be

A word: dragon

Great horned owl

Lion

Names bring

Moonlight on gravel

Dressed in silken scarves

A pirate's sword

And whisky

Glows in our skin

Halloween glow stick

Broke in his mouth

Floating like violet mercury

His lips bright from the car window

Quickly inside

Wash him then search

Trash for the label to read

The relieving word: non-toxic

The dump

The dump

Of any shit place

The plastic and washing

The glowing fluid I

Hold his mouth

Scared he won't

Look at me

Will there be fish to eat
One day
Breaking flesh
To feast
With a lightness
And assurance
Will our children
Have enough
An ancient question
And terror of not
Living up to what
The many tides of people
In us have made

I see him through a window
In the yard by the salvia
With a stick and wonder
What strangeness gave us
To see in the other
The likeness of our ways
How our acts speak
Through temporal spans
Now holding a pill bug
Inspecting the coiled density
Of the thing taking note
I wonder what it is
We are doing

And when it comes

To goodbye

No one survives

Except in memory

What we take

We keep inside

And tell again

The stories

Of an informing other

In us to let us

Be

Imagine him

As you one day too

The flesh gone to nothing

Scattered in some field

Of emptiness

A darkness through which

We go not

Alone but in them

So loved the world

Disappearing forever

A dream or so

It would seem

In that vanishing

Naked finger paints

Morning through a window

Willow and salvia bend in a moist

Southern breeze

We are watching

Each other and a painting

Arrives from sticky red-and-

Blue palms and fingers

One day nothing
Will happen of
Any importance
The birds will sing
The sun will do its thing
One day nothing
Will happen and
Shift silently
Through us

My sons play

In dirt and plastic

Toys lie sideways

A buzzard passes

Its shadow on the yard

I will tell them how it is

Like nothing we can know

So love remains

In images we carry

Of the dead and their words

Become our body

Of feeling

Keep going closer

To something out of reach

A god of ancient form

Long dead in a temple

Sacked by the children

Of a future no deity

Can apprehend

These hard days

Come along without warning

The car will not move

It obeys inert logic

Nature whose child in us

Haunts my habits of feeling

Cat in a window

He rides a limb as orange

Twilight lines the clouds

Reading *The Hobbit*

By candle

Gandalf arrives with adventures

He curls next to me

Warm in the sheets

Brother sleeping

Another room

An organ of sheetrock and lumber

Between us

What we see

Plays in the dance of

Shadows the room

Absorbs with us

Listening

Days vanish

Their morphology

Depends on

That

That

Sweet son

In his towel dripping

Water on the floor

Winter darkness out the window

Naked spine and shoulder

His wet hair

Sleepy he leans on me

And the sudden kiss

You hear in them
A voice or find
Some physical trope of
Surprise like the way
He holds his head or
Turns a phrase
The world is host
On the verge of ruin
The seas die
The land fries
And we move
Small on the husk of it
On that membrane
Make our words
All we are
In the world

New day

In the ways of new

Beings

Spinning in pistache

Shadows

As movement

Accumulates

By perceptive

Duration

Through my sons

To me enter

Anon

ACKNOWLEDGMENTS

Gratitude to Kirby for publishing "Sons" as a limited-edition chapbook for Knife Fork Book in 2017. "Everybody Ought to Treat a Stranger Right" and "Wreck on the Old Highway" appear in *Hambone* 23; thanks to editor Nathaniel Mackey for including them. A small portion of "April * Ontario" was published in the Ottawa-based journal *Touch the Donkey* in 2018; thanks to rob mclennan for this publication.

The quote by Ludwig Wittgenstein in "April * Ontario" is from *Tractatus Logico-Philosophicus* 6.4311 (1922). The full entry reads: "Death is not an event of life. Death is not lived through. If by eternity is understood not endless temporal duration but timelessness, then he lives eternally who lives in the present. Our life is endless in the way that our visual field is without limit."

Writing is a communal effort. Huge thanks to Mike Cavuto, Norma Cole, Sarah Henstra, Adam Katz, Kirby, Lauren Kirshner, Farid Matuk, Cecily Nicholson, Ruth Panofsky, and Alex Porco. Stephen Collis's generosity and attention to the work has been crucial to the final presentation. Stacy Blint helped realize the continental trajectory of the flying red horse. Hoa Nguyen and Roberto Tejada read late drafts of the opening essay: their conversations have been particularly vital. Catriona Strang devoted patience, clarity, and editorial guidance, for which I am grateful. Charles Olson, writing to Robert Duncan in 1953, equates form with love. "Doesn't it honestly – to be flat – come to, to love? that all springs up, there? And that what springs up is *energy* ..." Only that belief in form and love makes possible the force of relations here in the making of poetry.

Photo: Waylon Hart

A poet and literary scholar, **Dale Martin Smith** was born in Dallas, Texas. He is the author of the full-length poetry collections *Slow Poetry in America* (2014), *Black Stone* (2007), and *American Rambler* (2000). Smith's scholarly contributions include *Poets beyond the Barricade: Rhetoric, Citizenship, and Dissent after 1960* (2012) and two edited editions, *An Open Map: The Correspondence of Robert Duncan and Charles Olson* and *Imagining Persons: Robert Duncan's Lectures on Charles Olson* (both 2017), for which he received Simon Fraser University's Charles Olson Award. His essays and poetry have appeared in *Poetry*, the *Walrus*, the *Los Angeles Review of Books*, the *Boston Review*, and *Lambda Literary*. With Hoa Nguyen, he edited Skanky Possum, a book imprint and literary zine (1998–2004). Smith joined the faculty of English at Ryerson University in Toronto in 2011.